How to Write a Children's Picture Book

Volume III:
Figures of Speech

How to Write a Children's Picture Book

Volume III:
Figures of Speech

Learning from
Fish is Fish,
Lyle, Lyle, Crocodile,
Owen,
Caps for Sale,
Where the Wild Things Are,
and Other Favorite Stories

Eve Heidi Bine-Stock

E & E Publishing
Sausalito, California

E & E Publishing,
a Registered Trade Name of
THE E & E GROUP LLC
1001 Bridgeway, No. 227
Sausalito, California 94965
U.S.A.
Website: www.EandEGroup.com/Publishing
Email: EandEGroup@EandEGroup.com

Publisher's Cataloging-In-Publication Data
(Prepared by The Donohue Group, Inc.)

Bine-Stock, Eve Heidi.
    How to write a children's picture book / Eve Heidi
Bine-Stock.

    v. : ill. ; cm.

    Includes bibliographical references and indexes.
    Contents: v. 1. Structure -- v. 2. Word, sentence, scene,
story -- v. 3. Figures of speech.
    ISBN-13: 978-0-9719898-8-7 (v. 1)
    ISBN-10: 0-9719898-8-5 (v. 1)
    ISBN-13: 978-0-9748933-2-7 (v. 2)
    ISBN-10: 0-9748933-2-3 (v. 2)
    ISBN-13: 978-0-9748933-4-1 (v. 3)
    ISBN-10: 0-9748933-4-X (v. 3)

    1. Picture books for children--Technique. 2. Picture
books for children--Authorship. I. Title.

PN147.5 .B56
808/.06/8

Printed in U.S.A.

Acknowledgments

Many thanks to Dr. Gideon O. Burton, Professor of Rhetoric at Brigham Young University, for his thoughtful comments on this work. Dr. Burton is the author of *Silva Rhetoricae: The Forest of Rhetoric*, which may be accessed at http://rhetoric.byu.edu.

This work is dedicated to my loving husband, Edward, and his stream of sleepishness which provides the most unusual figures of speech. Fully awake, he provides unending support and encouragement. Every woman should be so fortunate.

Contents

Introduction

Many of us think of children's picture books as being written mostly with simple declarative sentences. What an eye-opener to learn that they are actually filled with delightful figures of speech.

I am *not* talking here about the common figures of speech we learn about in grade school: simile, onomatopoeia, alliteration, hyperbole and personification.

I am talking about more subtle and sophisticated figures of speech which we may not even recognize as figures at all (until they are pointed out to us), but their use gives stories a charm and freshness that stands up to repeated readings.

These figures have names which are eminently forgettable but the figures themselves make the stories in which they appear eminently memorable.

These figures are important for conveying nuanced meaning in a story, for giving characters a signature style, and for providing cohesion—the glue that binds parts of a story together.

It is therefore vital to become familiar with these figures—their names are secondary.

In this volume, I point out many figures which appear in masterworks of children's picture storybooks, so that they may be appreciated and savored, and their patterns emulated in your own work.

A note to the pedantic among us: for definitions of figures of speech, I have relied in good measure on *Figures of Speech* by Arthur Quinn[1]. He is the late Professor of Rhetoric at the University of California, Berkeley. I bring this up specifically because some others make very fine distinctions in their classification of figures of speech that are too fine to be of practical use to us in our examination and appreciation of children's picture storybooks.

---

[1] *Figures of Speech*. Arthur Quinn. Gibbs M. Smith, Inc., 1982.

Fish is Fish

by Leo Lionni

In this story, a fish yearns to see the world outside his pond that his friend the frog tells him about. The fish learns the hard way that "frogs are frogs and fish is fish."

Now, we all know that "fish is fish" is grammatically incorrect, yet we appreciate the charm and innocence of this utterance.

Rhetoricians call such an effective grammatical mistake an *enallage* (e-nal'-la-gee). More specifically, the phrase "fish is fish" is created by substituting the correct grammatical form of the verb *to be— are* in "fish are fish"—with the incorrect form, *is*, to create "fish is fish."

Had the author used the grammatically correct form, "fish are fish," the story would not be as delightful and memorable as it is.

Let us look at some other figures of speech in this story.

Repetition of Beginnings

The frog has a signature way of speaking that begins when he discovers that he has grown two little legs:

"Look," he said triumphantly. "Look, I am a frog."

When the frog regales his friend the fish with stories about the wonders he has seen outside the pond, the frog continues his signature way of speaking:

> "Birds," said the frog mysteriously. "Birds!" And he told the fish about the birds, who had wings, and two legs, and many, many colors.

> "Cows," said the frog. "Cows! They have four legs, horns, eat grass, and carry pink bags of milk."

Do you see the pattern in the above sentences? The author begins two sentences with *Look*; begins two sentences with *Birds*; begins two sentences with *Cows*. Rhetoricians call that kind of repetition *anaphora* (a-naph'-o-ra).
And then we read:

> "And people!" said the frog. "Men, women and children!" And he talked and talked until it was dark in the pond.

The frog does not repeat the word *people*, but he repeats the same idea *in other words*, and rhetoricians have a special word for that kind of repetition, too: *exergasia* (ex'-er-ga'-si-a).

Hark

Believe it or not, a woman standing next to me in a hotel once said to me, "Hark, the elevator is here." I must admit, until then I had only heard *Hark* together with "the herald angels sing." That woman used a figure of speech called *asterismos* (as-ter-is'-mos), which is the addition of a word or phrase to emphasize what follows.

The story *Fish is Fish* uses the same figure of speech when the fish remarks to himself about the wondrous things the frog has described:

> Ah, if he could only jump about like his friend and see that wonderful world.

The addition of that *Ah* emphasizes that which follows it.

Silence

Fish is Fish employs a very unusual figure of speech: the omission not of one letter, not of one word, but of *everything*. When a writer omits all words, there is only silence left. This figure of speech is called *reticentia* (re-ti-ken'-tee-a). About the only kind of story that can effectively employ such a figure of speech is the picture storybook. *Fish is Fish* employs silence during the two-page parade of marvelous creatures in the fish's imagination.

We shall see that there are other stories that use this figure of speech—this silence—as well.

Corduroy

by Don Freeman

Corduroy is the sweet story of a teddy bear waiting on a department store shelf for someone to take him home.

Repetition of "And"

When Corduroy goes in search of his lost button, he finds himself in the furniture department:

> [...] and there, before his eyes, was a most amazing sight—tables and chairs and lamps and sofas and rows and rows of beds.

The repeated use of all those *and*s is a particular kind of figure of speech called *polysyndeton* (pol'-y-syn'-de-ton). It makes the list seem as though it could go on forever. It also slows the pace of the sentence, lends a sense of grandeur, and, occasionally, as Arthur Quinn wrote[2], has "an almost hypnotic power."

---

[2] Page 12, *Figures of Speech*. Arthur Quinn. Gibbs M. Smith, Inc., 1982.

Repetition of Ends

As Corduroy journeys through the story, he makes discoveries and comments on them:

> "Could this be a mountain?" he wondered. I think I've always wanted to climb a mountain."

> "This must be a palace!" Corduroy gasped. "I guess I've always wanted to live in a palace."

> "This must be a bed," he said. "I've always wanted to sleep in a bed."

> "This must be home," he said. "I know I've always wanted a home!"

> "You must be a friend," said Corduroy. "I've always wanted a friend."

In each excerpt above, it is easy to see that the end of the first sentence is repeated at the end of the second sentence: mountain...mountain; palace...palace; bed...bed; home...home; friend...friend. This repetition of ends is a figure of speech called *epistrophe* (e-pis'-tro-phee). It provides resonance, cohesion and a sense of satisfaction.

Change in Usual Word Order

In Act II of *Corduroy*, during the bear's nocturnal adventure, we read:

—and up he went!

And up he crawled onto a large, thick mattress.

Off came the button....

—and off the mattress Corduroy toppled....

Over it fell with a crash!

In the above sentences, the usual order of words is changed; a single element, the adverb, is shifted to the beginning of the sentence, thereby shifting the stress to the beginning. Such a change in the usual order is a figure of speech called *hyperbaton* (hy-per'-ba-ton).

The hyperbaton is used only in Act II when Corduroy is searching for his button, exploring unknown territory, and getting into all kinds of mischief. We see that he is inquisitive, adventurous, spunky and, yes, *lively*. The repeated use of this figure of speech—which changes the usual word order—creates a special sentence rhythm that emphasizes Corduroy's special character.

Harry the Dirty Dog

by Gene Zion, illustrated by Margaret Bloy Graham

Harry the Dirty Dog is the story of a white dog with black spots who doesn't like baths *at all* until he gets so dirty that he turns into a black dog with white spots! To his chagrin, the family he lives with doesn't recognize him and it is only after he begs them to give him a bath that they realize he is really their Harry, after all.

Repetition in the Opposite Order

Probably the most memorable sentence in the whole book is:

> In fact, he changed from a white dog with black spots, to a black dog with white spots.

That is a particularly satisfying sentence, and one that brings out the contrast beautifully. How does it do that, exactly? By repeating words in the opposite order: AB, BA.

This figure of speech is known by two names: *antimetabole* (an-ti-me-tab'-o-lee) and *chiasmus* (kī-az'-mus).

This striking sentence is so key to the entire book that it is illustrated on the cover.

Another example of repeating words in the opposite order (AB, BA) is when Harry starts to do all his old, clever tricks:

He flip-flopped and he flop-flipped.

By repeatedly using this figure of speech, the author has added cohesion to the story and has also created a signature style.

Change in Usual Word Order

When Harry carries the scrubbing brush in his mouth and runs into the house, we read:

Up the stairs he dashed, with the family following close behind.

Here, the usual order of words is changed; a single element, the adverb, is shifted to the beginning of the sentence, thereby shifting the stress to the beginning. Such a change in the usual order is a figure of speech called *hyperbaton* (hy-per'-ba-ton).

Because of this figure of speech, that word *Up* receives an extra punch and we sense that we are at an important point in the story itself, which we are—Plot Twist II[3]—the turning point that leads to the resolution.

Addition of Letters to the End of a Word

When Harry jumps into the bathtub and sits up begging with the scrubbing brush in his mouth, the little girl cries:

"This little doggie wants a bath!"

The addition of *gie* to the end of *dog* conveys the ideas of both smallness and affection.

Adding letters like this to end of a word is the figure of speech called *proparalepsis* (pro'-par-a-lep'-sis). We are all familiar with this figure of speech and use it frequently in everyday life. Because of this, the use of it here in this book also adds realism and familiarity to the story.

---

3 Plot Twist II and the rest of the structure of this story is diagrammed in *How to Write a Children's Picture Book Volume I: Structure.* Eve Heidi Bine-Stock. E & E Publishing, 2004.

Immediate Repetition

As soon as the children started to scrub the doggie, they cried:

"It's Harry! It's Harry! It's Harry!"

That immediate repetition is a figure of speech called _epizeuxis_ (ep'-i-zeux'-is). It provides the strongest emphasis possible to what has just been said.

Lyle, Lyle, Crocodile

by Bernard Waber

This is the story of a sweet, friendly crocodile who is very happy living with the Primm family in their house in the city. But Lyle's presence makes his neighbor, Loretta the cat, miserable. Lyle wants desperately to win over Loretta, and her equally miserable owner, Mr. Grumps.

Immediate Repetition

The very title of this book is a rhyme that employs immediate repetition of Lyle's name. Such immediate repetition is a figure of speech called *epizeuxis* (ep'-i-zeux'-is). In this example, the immediate repetition helps to create a sing-song rhythm. In addition, repeating his name emphasizes Lyle as an individual who is more human that crocodile. The alternative, *Lyle the Crocodile*, would make Lyle more crocodile.

The repetition in the title also sets up expectations that the rest of the story will employ repetition—which indeed it does, as we shall see.

A One-Two Punch of Repetition

We know right away that we are reading a special story because it begins with figures of speech that create a one-two punch of repetition—first one kind of repetition, and then before we know it, a second kind of repetition.

> This is the house.
> The house on East 88th Street.
> Mr. and Mrs. Primm
> and their son Joshua
> live in the house
> on East 88th Street.

The end of the first sentence is repeated at the beginning of the following sentence fragment. This figure of speech is called *anadiplosis* (an'-a-di-plo'-sis). This ties the first sentence to what follows, and draws us into the story.

Then, the end of the sentence fragment is repeated at the end of the next sentence. This figure of speech is called *epistrophe* (e-pis'-tro-phee). It creates cohesion and a sense of satisfaction.

Taken together, these figures of speech turn the three first lines into a unified whole.

Also, by revealing information bit-by-bit, the author has created a mystery with the first sentence that is solved by the third sentence.

Repetition of Beginnings

A simple form of repetition that *Lyle, Lyle, Crocodile* employs is the repetition of a word or phase at or near the beginning of successive sentences:

> Mrs. Primm could spend hours just browsing around antique shops.
>
> Lyle could spend hours watching building construction.

And, when Mr. Gumps finally accepts Lyle, we read:

> "Hooray!" shouted the Primms.
> "Hooray!" shouted the crowd.

The repetition of beginnings is a figure of speech called *anaphora* (a-naph'-o-ra). Its use here emphasizes similarity.

Repetition of Ends

We have seen repetition of ends in this book before, and here it is again after Signor Valenti frees Lyle from the zoo and the showman says:

> "We'll fly to Australia. They'll love us in Australia."

Signor Valenti could just as well have said, "They'll love us there," without repeating the word *Australia*. But by repeating the word *Australia*, the author has emphasized that particular, far-away place. And in fact, Lyle's reaction confirms this interpretation: he groans and we read, "The very thought of never seeing the house on East 88th Street again was grim indeed and too much for him to endure."

The repetition of ends is a figure of speech called *epistrophe* (e-pis'-tro-phee).

Repetition of Beginning at the End

When Mr. Grumps arranges to have Lyle committed to the zoo, we see yet another form of repetition:

"The zoo!" Mrs. Primm exclaimed miserably, "whatever would Lyle be doing in the zoo?"

Here, the beginning of the sentence—*the zoo*—is repeated at the end of the sentence. This figure of speech is called *epanalepsis* (ep'-an-a-lep'-sis).

Mrs. Primm's first thought is *the zoo* and her last thought is *the zoo*; she is literally overwhelmed by the idea of the zoo.

Repetition in Other Words

You do not have to repeat the identical words in order to have a form of repetition; repetition *in other words* is still a form of repetition. For example, when Mrs. Primm is looking for Lyle in the department store, we read:

> "Excuse me," she said to the lady at the information booth, "have you seen a crocodile going past? He was wearing a red scarf."

> "No," answered the lady. "I have no information about a crocodile wearing a red scarf."

And next we read:

"Excuse me," said Mrs. Primm to the sporting goods salesman, "have you by chance come across a crocodile? His name is Lyle."

"Sorry, madam," answered the salesman, "I have not come across any crocodiles named Lyle today."

Repetition *in other words* is a figure of speech called *exergasia* (ex'-er-ga'-si-a). It is an effective way to emphasize something without being tedious—and enables you to inject humor as well, as it does here by drawing attention in a deadpan manner to the ludicrous nature of Mrs. Primm's questions.

Addition of Superfluous Words

A figure of speech that is a form of exaggeration is the addition of superfluous words. You can tell that they are superfluous because you can remove the excess words without changing the basic meaning of the sentence.

For example, when Mr. Grumps saw Lyle and Senor Valenti performing in the department store:

[...] he turned red, blue and purple with rage.

Now, one color would suffice. You could remove any two colors and still understand that Mr. Grumps was angry. But the addition of the superfluous words is used to convey the exaggerated nature of Mr. Grumps' anger.

In another example, after Lyle saves Mr. Grumps from the fire, Mr. Grumps says:

"Lyle is the bravest, kindest, most wonderful crocodile in the whole, wide world."

At the very least, you could remove *whole, wide* from the sentence and still retain the meaning. But having these words here creates an exaggeration that emphasizes Mr. Grumps' height of excitement and depth of gratitude.

Can you find other words that might be considered superfluous here? Hint: It would be most wonderful if you could.

Mr. Grumps is given a signature style of exaggerated emotions through the consistent use of superfluous words. It is no surprise that we are told that he is "even more excitable than his cat."

This figure of speech—the addition of superfluous words—is called *pleonasm* (plee'-o-nasm).

Sylvester and the Magic Pebble

by William Steig

In this touching story, a son and his parents suffer the anguish of separation and long to be reunited.

The trouble begins when Sylvester finds a magic pebble and is accidentally turned into a large rock. A year of anguish follows while Sylvester is separated from his loving parents. Then, come spring, when his parents set their picnic food upon the rock and sit down to eat, a chance encounter with the magic pebble turns Sylvester into himself again.

Addition of Superfluous Words

This book uses a figure of speech that we came across in *Lyle, Lyle, Crocodile*: the addition of superfluous words as a form of exaggeration.

When Sylvester turns into a rock before the very eyes of a lion, we read:

> The lion came bounding over, sniffed the rock a hundred times, walked around and around it, and went away

confused, perplexed, puzzled, and bewildered.

Let's look at those four adjectives, *confused, perplexed, puzzled,* and *bewildered.*
While each one has a slightly different shade of
meaning, you could remove any three and still
understand that the lion was befuddled.

Three of the adjectives are superfluous;
you can tell that they are superfluous because
you can remove the excess words without
changing the basic meaning of the sentence.

But adding superfluous adjectives here
creates the effect of exaggeration—in this case,
extreme befuddlement.

This figure of speech—the addition of
superfluous words—is called *pleonasm* (plee'-
o-nasm).

Repetition of Grammatical Forms

When Sylvester is turned into a rock and
he realizes that he cannot turn back into himself again, we read:

Being helpless, he felt hopeless.

While the sentiment is tragic, the sentence itself is remarkable for its satisfying
balance. *Helpless* and *hopeless* not only sound

similar, they have the same length and share the same grammatical form, being adjectives ending in *less*.

Another very important point is that the *el* in *helpless* has been substituted by the *o* in *hopeless*. This substitution of one part of a word—a sound or syllable—for another, is a figure of speech called *antisthecon* (an-tis′-the-con).

The repetition of forms creates the satisfying balance, and together with the word play of substitution, turns the sentence into a key moment that makes the sentence linger in our memory.

Omission of "And"

When Sylvester does not return home by morning, his parents go about inquiring of all the neighbors:

> They talked to all the children—the puppies, the kittens, the colts, the piglets.

We expect there to be at least one *and* in the list of children, but there isn't. Instead, there are just commas.

The effect is very subtle. Without an *and*, each item in the list is given equal emphasis, equal weight. Had there been an *and* before *the piglets,* there would have been a slight additional emphasis on *the piglets.* There also would have been a greater sense of finality.

Try reading that sentence again, this time adding *and* before *the piglets,* and you will see the difference.

Without the *and*s, there is also the sense that the children are being questioned all at once, rather than each type separately, which the accompanying picture confirms.

This figure of speech occurs again later in the story, when Sylvester's parents go for a picnic:

> Mr. Duncan walked aimlessly about while Mrs. Duncan set out the picnic food on the rock—alfalfa sandwiches, pickled oats, sassafras salad, timothy compote.

Without an expected *and,* each item in the list is given equal emphasis, equal weight. And there is less of a sense of finality to the sentence, and less of a sense of a particular order in which the food is set out.

The third time this figure of speech is used is near the very end, when Sylvester turns back into himself:

> You can image the scene that followed— the embraces, the kisses, the questions,

the answers, the loving looks, and the fond exclamations!

In this very long list, we might expect more than the lone *and* that appears at the end. If we had not become accustomed to this figure of speech through its prior use in the story, we might have expected to read something like this:

> You can image the scene that followed— the embraces and kisses, the questions and answers, the loving looks and fond exclamations!

But again, omitting expected *and*s in the original version has the effect of giving equal weight to each item on the list. Without the *and*s, we also get the sense that everything on the list is happening all at once, in a jumble.

The lone *and* in the original version that does appear before the last item on the list— *the fond exclamations!*—provides a sense of finality. And this is fitting since Sylvester is now finally himself again and finally reunited with his parents.

This figure of speech that we have been discussing—the omission of expected *and*s—is called *asyndeton* (a-syn'-de-ton).

Repetition by Negation

When all the dogs in Oakdale go searching for Sylvester, we read:

> They sniffed the rock of Strawberry Hill, but it smelled like a rock. It didn't smell like Sylvester.

Here, the same idea is repeated, once in the positive, and then again in the negative; first asserting something, and then presenting its contrary.

This figure of speech is called *antithesis* (an-tith'-e-sis). It has the advantage of giving a sense of completeness with only two items[4].

Repetition in the Opposite Order

After Sylvester is turned into a rock, much time passes. We read:

> Night followed day and day followed night over and over again.

This sentence conveys regularity and tedium[5]. But more than that. The first part of the

---

[4] Page 67, *Figures of Speech*. Arthur Quinn. Gibbs M. Smith, Inc., 1982.

sentence begins and ends with *night*, emphasizing the spiritual darkness that Sylvester finds himself in. It does all this by repeating words in the opposite order: AB, BA.

A lesser author might have written the following:

> Time passed—day after day, night after night, over and over again.

That is not nearly as effective as the original in conveying regularity, tedium and spiritual darkness.

The figure of speech that employs this AB, BA form is known by two names: *antimetabole* (an-ti-me-tab'-o-lee) and *chiasmus* (kī-az'-mus).

Omission

When winter comes, and Sylvester is still a rock on Strawberry Hill, we read:

> The winds blew, this way and that.

What is so special about this sentence? The second occurrence of the noun *way* has been omitted from the end, giving the sentence

---

5 The words *regularity* and *tedium* provided by Edward Z. Bine-Stock, Esq.

an elegant economy[6]. A less skilled author might have written:

> The winds blew, this way and that way.

The omission of the second *way* is a figure of speech called *ellipsis* (el-lip′-sis).

Repetition in Different Words

When Sylvester's parents go for a picnic on Strawberry Hill, his mother sits down on the rock, and her warmth wakes Sylvester from his deep winter sleep. He wants to shout to his parents. We read:

> But he couldn't talk. He had no voice. He was stone-dumb.

Here, the author has stated the same idea three times, but each time *in different words*. This kind of repetition creates emphasis of the main idea. There is also the sense that Sylvester has viewed the situation from every possible angle, and, try as he might, can find no solution to his predicament.

---

[6] The term *elegant economy* is from Page 27, *Figures of Speech*. Arthur Quinn. Gibbs M. Smith, Inc., 1982.

This kind of repetition—stating the same idea in different words—is a figure of speech called *exergasia* (ex'-er-ga'-si-a).

Where the Wild Things Are

by Maurice Sendak

In this story, young Max is sent to bed without his supper because he has been too wild. From his room, he journeys to the land of the Wild Things and becomes their king. After a wild rumpus there he tires and misses home. When he returns, he finds his supper waiting for him—and it is still hot.

Grammatical Mistake

After Max is sent to bed without his supper, a forest grows in his room and an ocean tumbles by with a private boat just for him:

> [...] and he sailed off through night and day and in and out of weeks and almost over a year to where the wild things are.

Near the end of the story, he returns the same way. He steps into his boat:

> [...] and sailed back over a year and in and out of weeks and through a day [...]

This is a very curious way to describe Max's voyage. Curious because the prepositions used are not the normal, expected ones. Our grammar teachers would tell us that we can:

- sail night and day
- sail for a night and a day
- sail through fog
- sail by moonlight
- sail through darkness
- sail for a week

but not:

- sail through night and day
- sail in and out of weeks
- sail over a year

By using the "incorrect" prepositions, the author has made time a physical entity that one can sail through, over, and in and out of. This heightens the imaginary nature of Max's voyage.

The author also appears to have taken the familiar idiom "week in and week out," and shuffled the words around to create "in and out of weeks"—an entirely new, fresh and memorable turn of phrase.

Rhetoricians call such an effective grammatical mistake—in this case, the incorrect use of prepositions—an *enallage* (e-nal'-la-gee).

Repetition

When Max comes to the place where the wild things are:

> they roared their terrible roars and gnashed their terrible teeth and rolled their terrible eyes and showed their terrible claws [...]

Here, the author has repeated many times the word *terrible*. This turn of phrase is known, appropriately, as *repetitio* (rep-e-tit'-ee-oe).

Far from thinking that the author is unimaginative, we get the sense that this is how Max—a young boy—would describe it.

Silence

Where the Wild Things Are employs a very unusual figure of speech: the omission of all words, leaving only silence. This figure of speech is called *reticentia* (re-ti-ken'-tee-a). This occurs during the six-page spread of illustrations showing the wild rumpus. The sound effects are left entirely to our imagination. About the only kind of story that can effectively employ such a figure of speech is the picture storybook.

Leo the Late Bloomer

by Robert Kraus,
illustrated by Jose Aruego

What a book! This deceptively simple story about a youngster who is slow to develop his skills, is filled with figures of speech. Perhaps this is one reason why we find it so pleasing to read again and again.

Repetition of Beginnings

When the story begins, we learn that Leo can't do anything right:

> He couldn't read.
> He couldn't write.
> He couldn't draw.

By the end of the story, Leo has bloomed, and now:

> He could read!
> He could write!
> He could draw!

The pattern in the above sentences is very clear to see. First, the sentences begin with

He couldn't, and later, the sentences begin with *He could*. This repetition of beginnings is a figure of speech called *anaphora* (a-naph'-o-ra). Its use emphasizes similarity. And here, it also sets up a rhythm.

Repetition of Ends

Since we have seen the repetition of beginnings, it will come as no surprise that *Leo the Late Bloomer* also employs the repetition of ends:

Every day Leo's father watched him for signs of blooming.

And every night Leo's father watched him for signs of blooming.

And:

The snows came.
Leo's father wasn't watching.
But Leo still wasn't blooming.

The trees budded.
Leo's father wasn't watching.
But Leo still wasn't blooming.

This repetition of ends is a figure of speech called *epistrophe* (e-pis'-tro-phee).

Here, the repetition creates a sameness that emphasizes the unchanging nature of Leo's condition.

Hark

At the end of the litany of things that Leo cannot do, we read:

And, he never said a word.

The addition of that *And,* emphasizes what follows.

Then, at the end of the story, after Leo blooms, he also speaks, and it isn't just a word, it is a whole sentence. We read:

And that sentence was...
"I made it!"

Here, the phrase *And that sentence was...* emphasizes what follows.

This figure of speech—the addition of a word or phrase to emphasize what follows—is called *asterismos* (as-ter-is'-mos). We are all familiar with this figure of speech; just recall, "Hark, the herald angels sing."

Special Repetition Often Used in Aphorisms

When Leo's parents speak, they use a figure of speech that is common in aphorisms:

"What's the matter with Leo?" asked Leo's father.

"Nothing," said Leo's mother. "Leo is just a late bloomer."

"Better late than never," thought Leo's father.

What, exactly, is the figure of speech that is being used here? To answer that, let us take a look at the word *late*. When Leo's mother uses it, it acts as an adjective; when Leo's father uses it, it acts as an adverb.

It is easier to see this if we fill in the words missing from *Better late than never*: "Better to bloom late than never to bloom at all."[7] Now it is clear that *late* is an adverb when Leo's father uses it.

The repetition of a word or root in different grammatical functions or forms is a

---

[7] The omission of all these words from the original phrase is a figure of speech called *ellipsis* (el-lip'-sis).

figure of speech called *polyptoton* (po-lyp'-toe-ton).

Another example of this figure of speech occurs later in the story:

"Are you sure Leo's a bloomer?"
asked Leo's father.

"Patience," said Leo's mother.
"A watched bloomer doesn't bloom."

Here, the root *bloom* is used in two different grammatical forms: once in a noun, and then again in a verb.

Arthur Quinn tell us[8] that this figure of speech—the polyptoton—"is used frequently in aphorisms, probably because it is rarely recognized as a figure at all and hence the phrase is more likely to be experienced as strikingly original."

---

[8] Page 74, *Figures of Speech*. Arthur Quinn. Gibbs M. Smith, Inc., 1982.

Owen

by Kevin Henkes

In this story, little Owen loves his fuzzy yellow blanket and takes it with him everywhere. The meddling neighbor, Mrs. Tweezers, tells Owen's parents that he is too old for this and gives advice on how to take Fuzzy away from Owen. Yet Owen thwarts his parents' every attempt to take Fuzzy away, until one day his mother comes up with a solution that makes everybody happy.

An Adjective Used as a Noun & Other Substitutions of One Part of Speech for Another

The story begins with this sentence:

Owen had a fuzzy yellow blanket.

Later, on page two, we read:

"Fuzzy goes where I go," said Owen.

There has been a subtle change here: _fuzzy_ is first used as an adjective (_fuzzy yellow_ *blanket*), and then used as a noun—a proper noun, no less: *Fuzzy*.

Put another way, instead of saying something like:

"Blankie goes where I go,"

where the noun *blankie* is used, Owen uses the adjective *fuzzy* as though it were a noun:

"Fuzzy goes where I go," said Owen.

The author has substituted one part of speech for another, a figure of speech called *anthimeria* (an'-thi-me'-ree-a).

It's just a hop, skip and a jump from this anthimeria to others in literature for grown-ups:

> he sang his didn't he danced his did
> - Cummings

> I am going in search of the great perhaps.
> - Rabelais

> Every why hath a wherefore.
> - Shakespeare

Little Owen is a budding Shakespeare!

Triple Threat: Omission of Subject, Verb and Conjunction "And"

Let us pick up where we left off and see what other figures of speech the author has in store for us:

"Fuzzy goes where I go," said Owen.
And Fuzzy did.
Upstairs, downstairs, in-between.
Inside, outside, upside down.

The last two sentences are hardly sentences at all; both the subject and verb are missing! What's left is just a list of adverbs. But we are not confused because we understand from the context what is missing. A grammatically "proper" version would be:

They went upstairs, downstairs, in-between...

The general term for the omission of a word or phrase is *ellipsis* (el-lip′sis).

What is also striking here is the absence of the connecting word *and* in the list, a figure of speech called *asyndeton* (a-syn′-de-ton).

Pared down to the essentials, the author's original sentence fragments create a rhythm. We also get the sense that there is no particular order to where Fuzzy and Owen go, and that they go to these places over and over again.

Another example of these two figures of speech follows immediately in the story:

> "Fuzzy likes what I like," said Owen.
> And Fuzzy did.
> Orange juice, grape juice, chocolate milk.
> Ice cream, peanut butter, applesauce cake.

Both the subject and verb are missing again. When we fill them in, we see that the grammatically "proper" version might be:

> They liked orange juice, grape juice, chocolate milk...

Again, pared down to the essentials, these sentence fragments create a rhythm. And we sense that Owen and Fuzzy enjoy these foods over and over again, in no particular order.

Addition of Superfluous Words

The meddling neighbor, Mrs. Tweezers, thinks Owen is too old to be carrying Fuzzy around with him. She explains to Owen's parents how to use the Blanket Fairy as a ruse to take Fuzzy away from Owen while he is asleep. We read:

> That night Owen's parents told Owen to put Fuzzy under his pillow. In the morning Fuzzy would be gone, but the Blanket Fairy would leave an absolutely wonderful, positively perfect, especially terrific big-boy gift in its place.

Oh, my! Could that gift get any better?

The addition of superfluous words—in this case adjectives—is a figure of speech called *pleonasm* (plee'-o-nasm). And a fine figure of speech it is because all those adjectives serve to exaggerate the value of the gift.

You can tell that most of the adjectives are superfluous because you can remove the excess ones without changing the basic meaning of the sentence.

We come across this figure of speech again near the end of the story. After Owen has foiled his parents' every attempt to take Fuzzy away from him, we read:

> And then suddenly Owen's mother said, "I have an idea!" It was an absolutely wonderful, positively perfect, especially terrific idea.

Now, after all the *Sturm und Drang* we've been through, this figure of speech does not appear to be an exaggeration at all!

Repetition of Beginnings

Back to the Blanket Fairy.

Before going to sleep, Owen stuffs Fuzzy inside his pajama pants:

> "No Blanket Fairy," said Owen in the morning.
> "No kidding," said Owen's mother.
> "No wonder," said Owen's father.

The word *No* is repeated at the beginning of each sentence. The *No*s of Owen's parents counter the *No* of Owen, emphasizing the standoff. Furthermore, the similar structure of the two sentences involving his parents emphasizes their united front. We see this united front again when Owen demands to bring Fuzzy to school:

> "No," said Owen's mother.
> "No," said Owen's father.

The repetition of beginnings is a figure of speech called anaphora (a-naph'-o-ra).

Opposing Statements

At one point, Owen's mother and father attempt to convince Owen to give up Fuzzy by reasoning with him:

"Fuzzy's dirty," said Owen's mother.
"Fuzzy's torn and ratty," said Owen's father.
"No," said Owen. "Fuzzy is perfect."
And Fuzzy was.

Here are two sentences stating what is wrong with Fuzzy balanced by two sentences affirming the opposite. A beautiful example of the figure of speech called *antithesis* (an-tith'-e-sis). The balance gives the passage a sense of completeness.

Omission of Subject (Again)

The meddling neighbor, Mrs. Tweezers, has a signature way of speaking. At two different points in the story we read:

"Can't be a baby forever," said Mrs. Tweezers.

And:

"Can't bring a blanket to school," said Mrs. Tweezers.

Mrs. Tweezers omits the subject in both sentences.

We have already learned that the general term for the omission of a word or phrase is *ellipsis* (el-lip'sis).

Here, we could add *Owen* or *He* or *One* or *A Child* to the sentences in order to make them grammatical.

By omitting the subject, Mrs. Tweezers implies *both* that Owen specifically, and all children in general (including yours), can't be a baby forever, and can't bring a blanket to school.

Repetition of Beginning at the End

After Owen's father dips Owen's favorite corner of Fuzzy into vinegar, we read:

Owen sniffed it and smelled it and sniffed it.

Here, words near the beginning of the sentence—*sniffed it*—are repeated at the end of the sentence. This figure of speech is called *epanalepsis* (ep'-an-a-lep'-sis). It creates a balanced and closed unit that "tends to make the sentence or clause in which it occurs stand apart from its surroundings"[9], focusing our attention on it.

Repetition in Specific and General Sense

In an effort to rid Fuzzy of the vinegar smell, Owen rubs Fuzzy all around his sandbox and buries it in the garden and digs it up again. Fuzzy is now good as new except:

Fuzzy wasn't very fuzzy anymore.

Here, the word *fuzzy* is used in two different senses: first to refer specifically to the blanket, and then to refer to its general quality of fuzziness. This is a figure of speech call *ploce* (ploe'-see).

Immediate Repetition

When Owen's mother has a bright idea for solving the problem of how to take the blanket away from Owen without his complaining, we read:

---

[9] Page 89, *Figures of Speech*. Arthur Quinn. Gibbs M. Smith, Inc., 1982.

Snip, snip, snip.
Sew, sew, sew.
"Dry your eyes."
"Wipe your nose."
Hooray, hooray, hooray!

The immediate repetition we see here is a figure of speech called *epizeuxis* (ep'-i-zeux'-is). In this example, the immediate repetition (beginning with *snip, snip, snip*) helps to create a crisp rhythm that is developed into a poem. In the last sentence—the cheer—the immediate repetition provides the strongest emphasis possible to what has been written.

Caps for Sale

by Esphyr Slobodkina

In this story, a peddler takes a break from an unsuccessful morning selling caps. He takes a nap under a tree and when he awakes, he finds that a troop of monkeys in the tree has stolen all but one of his caps. How the peddler finally retrieves his caps is the surprise ending to this story.

Overflowing as this story is with figures of speech, we shall look at only a selection of them.

Omission of Subject and Verb

The very title of the book, *Caps for Sale,* and the peddler's chant:

> "Caps! Caps for Sale!
> Fifty cents a cap!"

are figures of speech. Both the subject and the verb are missing but we can easily fill them in from the context:

> I have caps! I have caps for sale!
> They cost fifty cents a cap!

However, we do not expect a peddler to call out such complete, grammatically correct sentences, and the use of this figure of speech here authentically captures the peddler's chant.

The general term for the omission of a word or phrase is *ellipsis* (el-lip'sis).

<u>Opposing Statements</u>

At the beginning of the story we are told that the peddler

...was not like an ordinary peddler carrying his wares on his back. He carried them on top of his head.

We can look at this passage in a couple of different ways. One way is to say that first the negative is stated (he is not an ordinary peddler) and then the positive is implied (he is unique).

Another way to look at it is, first one idea is stated (carrying wares on the back) and then a contrasting idea is stated (carrying wares on top of the head).

Either way you look at it, one idea is stated and then its contrary or opposing idea is stated.

This is a figure of speech is called *antithesis* (an-tith'-e-sis). It has the advantage of giving a sense of completeness with only two items[10].

Addition of Superfluous Words

One morning, the peddler tries to sell his caps. We read:

> He walked up the street and he walked down the street calling, "Caps! Caps for sale. Fifty cents a cap."

Instead, the author could easily have written:

> He walked up and down the street calling...

We can see that the author added superfluous words to his version, a figure of speech called *pleonasm* (plee'-o-nasm). You can tell that they are superfluous because you can remove the excess words without changing the basic meaning of the sentence.

In this case, the addition of these words draws out the time it takes us to read the

---

[10] Page 67, *Figures of Speech*. Arthur Quinn. Gibbs M. Smith, Inc., 1982.

sentence and give us a better sense of the time it takes the peddler to walk up and down the street. The repetition also provides a sense of the monotony that the peddler feels.

Repetition in Other Words

What does the peddler get for all his efforts? We read:

> But nobody wanted any caps
> that morning. Nobody wanted
> even a red cap.

Here we have a form of repetition: the same idea is repeated *in other words*, a figure of speech called *exergasia* (ex'-er-ga'-si-a). It is an effective way to emphasize something without being tedious.

And that word *even* serves as punctuation to let us know we have come to the end of this segment of the story.

Change in Usual Word Order

The peddler decides to take a break from his unsuccessful morning of selling. We read:

"I think I'll go for a walk in the country,"
said he.

Today we are so accustomed to reading
he said—rather than *said he*—that we come to
expect it. So when we read these words in a
different order, *said he*, it sounds both fresh
and archaic at the same time. It helps to set the
story in an earlier time.

This figure of speech also occurs later in
the story, after the peddler has walked for a
long time and comes to a great big tree:

That's a nice place for a rest,"
thought he.

The general term for any deviation from
the expected word order is called *hyperbaton*
(hy-per'-ba-ton).

Immediate Repetition

Let us back up a bit and pick up the
story again when the peddler decides to go for a
walk in the country:

And he walked out of town—
slowly, slowly,
so as not to upset his caps.

The immediate repetition of the word *slowly* is a figure of speech called *epizeuxis* (ep'-i-zeux'-is).

The repetition emphasizes what has just been said—it emphasizes slowness. We even find ourselves drawing out the words so that we read them slowly in imitation.

Step-like Repetition & Addition of "Or"

After the peddler awakes from his nap under a tree, he finds that all but one of his caps are gone. After he looks all around the tree, he finally looks up and what does he see?

> On every branch sat a monkey. On every monkey was a grey, or a brown, or a blue, or a red cap!

The end of the first sentence (*monkey*) is repeated near the beginning of the following sentence. This figure of speech is called *ana-diplosis* (an'-a-di-plo'-sis).

One effect this has is to emphasize the repeated words. Also, as one link in a chain is tied to the next, this figure ties the first sentence to the next, and draws us into the scene.

There is another figure of speech at play here too: The repeated use of all those *or*s is called *paradiastole* (par'-a-di-as'-to-lee). It makes the list seem as though it could go on forever. This figure can also be used with other disjunctives such as *either, neither, nor*.

(Note: some classification schemes reserve the term *paradiastole* for an entirely different figure of speech which is not dealt with in this volume.)

Harold and the Purple Crayon

by Crocket Johnson

In this story, little Harold goes for a walk in the moonlight, drawing on help from his trusty purple crayon to make the moon and everything else that appears during his adventures.

Repetition of Ends

The story begins with:

One evening, after thinking it over for some time, Harold decided to go for a walk in the moonlight. There wasn't any moon, and Harold needed a moon for a walk in the moonlight.

By repeating the phrase *a walk in the moonlight*, the author has emphasized that particular aspect of the story. In fact, the entire story is about a walk in the moonlight.

This repetition of ends is a figure of speech called *epistrophe* (e-pis'-tro-phee).

Repetition of Beginning at the End

Immediately after Harold draws a moon for his walk in the moonlight, we read:

> He made a long straight path so he wouldn't get lost. And he set off on his walk, taking his big purple crayon with him. But he didn't seem to be getting anywhere on the long straight path.

When the beginning of a passage is repeated at the end of the passage, it is a figure of speech called *epanalepsis* (ep'-an-a-lep'-sis).

This figure creates a balanced and closed unit that "tends to make the sentence or [passage] in which it occurs stand apart from its surroundings"[11].

This figure of speech also gives us the sense that we have come to the end of this particular subject—and we have: Harold now leaves the long straight path for a short cut across a field.

A Part Representing the Whole

The story continues:

---

[11] Page 89, *Figures of Speech*. Arthur Quinn. Gibbs M. Smith, Inc., 1982.

The short cut led to where Harold thought a forest ought to be. He didn't want to get lost in the woods. So he made a very small forest, with just one tree in it.

Here, Harold has made one tree to symbolize an entire forest—the part represents the whole.

When a sentence uses a part to represent the whole (*all hands on deck* instead of *all sailors on deck*), or uses the whole to represent a part (*here comes the law* instead of *here comes a cop*), it is a figure of speech called *synecdoche* (syn-ek'-do-kee).

Harold has created a visual synecdoche!

Substitution of Word by Related Word

Harold's tree turns out to be an apple tree. We read:

The apples would be very tasty, Harold thought, when they got red.

This sentence is very interesting because usually we talk in terms of an apple getting *ripe*, not *red*. The author has used a word related to ripe, rather than ripe itself, a figure of speech called *metonymy* (me-ton'-y-mee).

This is a particularly apt choice of word for a children's book since *red* is more easily understood by a young child than *ripe*. Besides that, it is a new way to convey an old concept.

A One-Two Punch

The story of the apple tree continues:

So he put a frightening dragon under the tree to guard the apples. It was a terribly frightening dragon. It even frightened Harold.

The author first writes *a frightening dragon* and then writes *a terribly frightening dragon*. The addition of the *terribly* the second time serves to amplify the frightening quality. Fittingly enough, this is a rhetorical strategy called *amplification*.

The author also repeats the root *frighten*, using it first in the adjective *frightening* and then in the verb *frightened*.

The repetition of a word or root in different grammatical functions or forms is a figure of speech called *polyptoton* (po-lyp'-toe-ton).

That is one scary dragon!

Change in Usual Word Order

At one point in his adventures, Harold looks for a hill to climb, to see where he is:

> Harold knew that the higher up he went, the farther he could see. So he decided to make the hill into a mountain.

Now, we have all heard of *to make a mountain out of a molehill*. The author has changed the expected word order of this familiar phrase to create *make the hill into a mountain*. This is an inside joke that young children will likely not understand but adults will appreciate.

The general term for any deviation from the expected word order is called *hyperbaton* (hy-per'-ba-ton).

One Verb Applied to Two Nouns

Harold falls off the mountain:

> But, luckily, he kept his wits and his purple crayon.

This sentence strikes us as especially clever when we read it. How did the author accomplish this? By applying one verb, *kept,* to two nouns, *wit* and *crayon.*

This figure of speech is called *zeugma* (zeug'-ma).

Another One-Two Punch

Later in the story, when Harold tries to think where his bedroom window ought to be, we read:

He made a big building full of windows.
He made lots of building full of windows.
He made a whole city full of windows.

Harold has gotten carried away in his attempts to find his bedroom window. In fact, it seems as though he has temporarily forgotten his main goal and has gotten caught up in the act of drawing windows for the sake of drawing them.

The progression from smaller to larger (from one building, to lots of buildings, to a whole city) is a figure of speech called *auxesis* (aux-ee'-sis).

There is another figure of speech in play here as well. Both the beginnings and the ends of the sentences are repeated, a figure called *symploce* (sym-plo'kee).

Double Entendre

At one point in his adventures, Harold sails in a trim little boat. Then we read:

> After he had sailed long enough, Harold made land without much trouble.

Here, the word *made* has two meanings: Harold both reaches the shore and draws it with his crayon. This is a figure of speech called *double entendre* (duhb'-uhl ahn-tahn'-druh).

We see this figure again in the story:

> And then Harold made his bed. He got in it and he drew up the covers.

Here, both *made* and *drew* have double meanings. Thanks to the author's clever word play, we never tire of reading these sentences.

Repetition in Different Senses

With Harold now in bed, we reach the end of the story:

> The purple crayon dropped on the floor. And Harold dropped off to sleep.

This is another brilliant example of word play: the word *dropped* is repeated in the same grammatical form, but in two different senses, a figure of speech called *antanaclasis* (ant'-an-a-cla'-sis).

The story ends on a high note, with the reader savoring the author's tour de force.

Bibliography

Caps for Sale: A Tale of a Peddler, Some Monkeys and Their Monkey Business. Esphyr Slobodkina. Harper & Row, 1947.

Corduroy. Don Freeman. Viking Press, 1968.

Figures of Speech. Arthur Quinn. Gibbs M. Smith, 1982.

Fish is Fish. Leo Lionni. Pantheon, 1970.

Harold and the Purple Crayon. Crockett Johnson. Harper & Row, 1955.

Harry the Dirty Dog. Gene Zion. Illustrated by Margaret Bloy Graham. Harper, 1956.

Leo the Late Bloomer. Robert Kraus. Illustrated by Jose Aruego. Windmill Books, 1971.

Lyle, Lyle, Crocodile. Bernard Waber. Houghton Mifflin, 1965.

Owen. Kevin Henkes. Greenwillow, 1993.

Sylvester and the Magic Pebble. William Steig. Windmill Books, 1969.

Where the Wild Things Are. Maurice Sendak. Harper & Row, 1963.

Glossary/Index

amplification (am'-pli-fi-ca'-tion)
  enlarging or expanding an idea

  So he put a frightening dragon under the tree to guard the apples. It was a terribly frightening dragon.

  See page 72.

anadiplosis (an'-a-di-plo'-sis)
  The end of one sentence is repeated at the beginning of the next.

  This is the house.
  The house on East 88th Street.

  See pages 24, 66.

anaphora (a-naph'-o-ra)
  repetition of beginnings

  "Hooray!" shouted the Primms.
  "Hooray!" shouted the crowd.

  See pages 12, 25, 46, 56.

antanaclasis (ant'-an-a-cla'-sis)
A word is repeated in the same grammatical form, but in two different senses.

> The purple crayon dropped on the floor.
> And Harold dropped off to sleep.

See page 76.

anthimeria (an'-thi-me'-ree-a)
One part of speech is substituted for another.

> "Fuzzy goes where I go."

See page 52.

antimetabole (an-ti-me-tab'-o-lee)
Words are repeated in the opposite order: AB, BA.

> In fact, he changed from a white dog with black spots, to a black dog with white spots.

See pages 20, 37.

antisthecon (an-tis'-the-con)
substitution of one part of a word—a sound or syllable—for another

Being helpless, he felt hopeless.

See page 33.

antithesis (an-tith'-e-sis)
An idea is repeated, first asserting something, and then presenting its contrary.

It smelled like a rock. It didn't smell like Sylvester.

See pages 36, 57, 63.

asterismos (as-ter-is'-mos)
addition of a word or phrase to emphasize what follows

And that sentence was...
"I made it!"

See pages 13, 47.

asyndeton (a-syn'-de-ton)
omission of expected *and*s

They went upstairs, downstairs, in-between.

See pages 35, 53.

auxesis (aux-ee'-sis)
progression from smaller to larger or from lesser to greater importance

He made a big building full of windows.
He made lots of building full of windows.
He made a whole city full of windows.

See page 74.

chiasmus (kī-az'-mus)
another name for antimetabole

double entendre
(duhb'-uhl ahn-tahn'-druh)
one word has two meanings

See page 75.

ellipsis (el-lip'-sis)
omission

The winds blew, this way and that.

See pages 38, 53, 58, 62.

enallage (e-nal'-la-gee)
an effective grammatical mistake

Fish is Fish

See pages 11, 43.

epanalepsis (ep'-an-a-lep'-sis)
The beginning of the sentence is repeated at the end of the sentence.

"The zoo!" Mrs. Primm exclaimed miserably, "whatever would Lyle be doing in the zoo?"

See pages 27, 58, 70.

epistrophe (e-pis'-tro-phee)
repetition of ends

"We'll fly to Australia. They'll love us in Australia."

See pages 16, 24, 26, 47, 69.

epizeuxis (ep'-i-zeux'-is)
immediate repetition

Hooray, hooray, hooray!

See pages 22, 23, 60, 66.

exergasia (ex'-er-ga'-si-a)
repetition in other words

"And people!" said the frog. "Men, women and children!"

See pages 13, 28, 39, 64.

hyperbaton (hy-per'-ba-ton)
a change in the usual word order

Over it fell with a crash!

See pages 17, 20, 65, 73.

metonymy (me-ton'-y-mee)
use of a related word rather than the word itself

The apples would be very tasty, Harold thought, when they got red.

See page 71.

paradiastole (par'-a-di-as'-to-lee)
repeated use of disjunctives (or, nor, either, neither)

On every monkey was a grey, or a brown, or a blue, or a red cap!

See pages 66, 67.

(Note: some classification schemes reserve the term *paradiastole* for an entirely different figure of speech which is not dealt with in this volume.)

pleonasm (plee'-o-nasm)
addition of superfluous words

In the morning Fuzzy would be gone, but the Blanket Fairy would leave an absolutely wonderful, positively perfect, especially terrific big-boy gift in its place.

See page 30, 32, 55, 63.

ploce (ploe'-see)
use of a word in two different senses: first specifically, then generally

Fuzzy wasn't very fuzzy anymore.

See page 59.

polyptoton (po-lyp'-toe-ton)
repetition of a word or root in different grammatical functions or forms

"A watched bloomer doesn't bloom."

See pages 49, 72.

polysyndeton (pol'-y-syn'-de-ton)
repeated use of conjunctions (the word *and*)

[...] and there, before his eyes, was a most amazing sight—tables and chairs and lamps and sofas and rows and rows of beds.

See page 15.

proparalepsis (pro'-par-a-lep'-sis)
addition of letters to the end of a word

"This little doggie wants a bath!"

See page 21.

reticentia (re-ti-ken'-tee-a)
omission of everything

See page 14, 43.

symploce (sym-plo'kee)
repetition of both the beginnings and the ends of a sentence

He made a big building full of windows.
He made lots of building full of windows.
He made a whole city full of windows.

synecdoche (syn-ek'-do-kee)
use of a part to represent the whole (*all hands on deck* instead of *all sailors on deck*), or the whole to represent a part (*here comes the law* instead of *here comes a cop*)

See page 71.

zeugma (zeug'-ma)
applying one verb to two nouns

But, luckily, he kept his wits and his purple crayon.

See page 74.

About the Author

Eve Heidi Bine-Stock is the author of Volumes I, II and III of this series, *How to Write a Children's Picture Book*, and has written pseudonymously numerous books for children. Ms. Bine-Stock is also the Publisher of **E & E Publishing** which publishes children's picture books and non-fiction books for adults.

CPSIA information can be obtained at www.ICGtesting.com
Printed in the USA
LVOW06s2313200714

395187LV00001BA/76/P